ANOTHER SHORE

ANOTHER SHORE

Poems by

James Dott

Kelsay Books

Copyright 2019 James Dott. All rights reserved.
This material may not be reproduced in any form,
published, reprinted, recorded, performed,
broadcast, rewritten or redistributed
without the explicit permission of James Dott.
All such actions are strictly prohibited by law.

Cover design: Shay Culligan

ISBN: 978-1-949229-96-7

Kelsay Books Inc.

kelsaybooks.com
502 S 1040 E, A119
American Fork, Utah 84003

ANOTHER SHORE

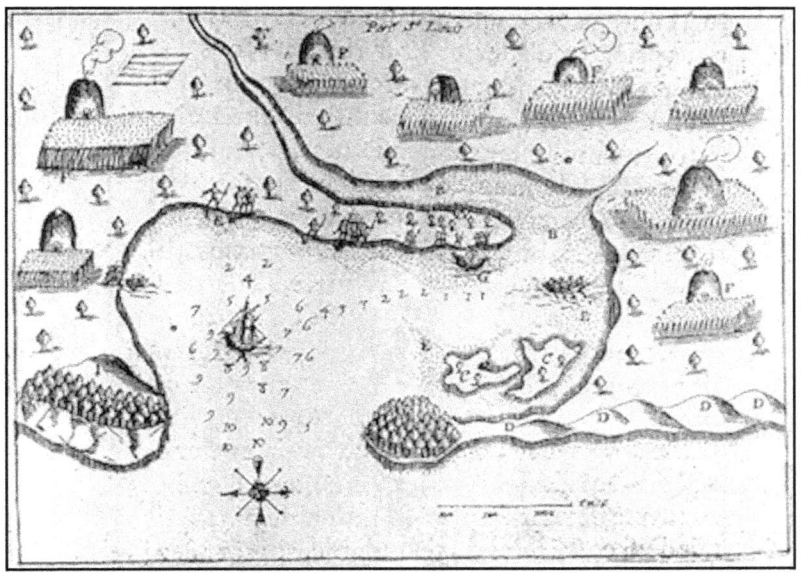

"And the end of all our exploring
Will be to arrive where we started
And know the place for the first time"
—T.S. Eliot

*Patuxet Village/Plimoth Plantation
Massachusetts
1620s*

For my family

Acknowledgments

I would like to give my deepest thanks to my wife, Ann, and daughter, MeiLi, for their loving support, and to my friend and fellow poet, Karin Temple, for her guidance and encouragement with this project. Thanks also to my friends and writers at Ric's Mic in Astoria who listened and responded to these poems.

My thanks to the editors and staffs of the journals where these poems were first published:

"Arrival" in *Turtle Island Quarterly*

"Fetching Water" in *The Blue Heron Review*

"The Fire" in *Rain*

Contents

Arrival	15
In the Beech Grove	17
First Winter	19
Embers	21
Signs	23
Visions, Voices	25
Fetching Water	27
Undertow	29
Prodigal Daughter	32
Only Her Shoes	36
Before First Light	38
Return	40
Into Wilderness	44
Rumors	46
Basketry	47
In Raven's Dream	50
The Fire	53

Arrival

No Middle Passage, a chosen voyage,
only one death,
yet no small test of faith,
the crowded stench
unbathed bodies, their wastes,
lice, weevils, fouled water,
the sailors' taunting curses,
it was one of them who died
as you sow so shall you reap,
the pitch and wallow
in weeks of heaving storm swell

A moonless night,
scattered stars, frost on rigging, the cry, *land,*
a lighter band above the darker sea
distant hiss of waves on sand
a prayer for this the promised shore

With morning they rowed to shore
younger children ran the beach
she walked the dune ridge
to an ice-rimmed pond
white swans took flight,
she stopped,
turned seaward, slid down,
dug a bowl in the sand
water welled up
she dipped a finger
licked
fresh not salt
then the voice
from behind her left shoulder

I am your source, your spring
grasp me, I will slip away
immerse in me, I will float you
I will be the stream that delivers you
to your final ocean
drink of me

She cupped her hands,
they filled, she lifted them
she drank

In the Beech Grove

Summer, Devonshire

How was it
that it was the mother
who stepped from stone to stone across the brook
meandered from the chalk cliff
through the beech wood dell
the mother who plunged her aching feet
into the soothing pool

How was it
that it was the daughter
who remembered the sweltering Sabbath trek
the rutted road, the dusty path
the cool and dappled dusk within the grove
the daughter not yet born but present
within her mother's burgeoned womb

How was it that
she could hear the reverend's sermon
echo off the cliff
the elders' stern affirms
a distant buzz of insects

How was it that she could feel
the smooth trunk against my spine
how it held me
not as a wall would prop a hoe
but as my husband's hand would press
easing weariness
and how his other hand would gather both of mine

And how was it that she saw,
when I looked up, the deep canopy of green
and heard, through the shifting slur of leaves,

a thrush's song and then
that shaded voice so close to murmur
I was not certain I had heard it
until she spoke again the words:

Do as I
draw what's holy
into your heart
and let it rise

First Winter

Hands cupped tightly
still the water slips away

Lapped curves of foam
sink in sand

At first the promise held
despite their late arrival,
the scurvy and the cold
despite their being
as children to this place
knowing so little of
the lay of land,
where the currents drew,
what weather a wind would bring,
the names and ways of the others
who had dwelt there for so long

Sleet and snow on frozen ground
vapor hovers
above the spring's frost-lipped mouth

In the pit of winter
a pestilence ran amok
so many dying
some days two or three
until only half remained
whole families gone
parents lost children
wives lost husbands, husbands their wives
she: mother and father,
her brother, both sisters
all flown

Day dwindles
crows breathe up from abandoned fields
others spew over the hill
converge
calling, cawing
sudden diminuendo
the flock spills apart
soaked in the dark

Far south
the sun bursts
orange out of the sea's peened pewter
ship's spars catch fire
memory of warmth treasures her cheeks

An approaching squall
turns the east to night
breaker foam blown west
a wedge of swans beats north
fully lit in a band of light
between her and the storm
no gust has touched them yet
she listens for their calls

Instead that voice
so close, confiding:
abide in this
nothing holds you
nothing for you to hold
your wind is here
open your wings
now glide

Embers

The last candle stutters,
weariness washes her nearer sleep,
but ice already on the kettle,
the blanket again too thin
the fire banked in hope of morning
its embers coveting
their shrinking pools of molten red
behind, beneath,
only black begetting black

Once more the riddles surface from the deep

Where had that breath flown from
to glide, to hover above the waters' face?
What came before the thought took tongue
and sparked the word that swarmed
the darkened hearth with flame?

A ripple of reply,
Call it naught,
call it empty void, or
hollow hole,
so cold

All things
each room, its walls,
each wall, its wood
each wood, its tree
each tree, its wilderness
each drop, its wave
each wave, its sea
each reflected star, its firmament

*So cold
all these
and every other
so cold
shall be slowed,
squeezed down
to nothing*

Signs

They came to her,
leaves blown,
pressed to her breast
then swept on

The pile of stones
among the weeds
in the old field,
for the dead boys
to throw at crows

A turtle traced
in the dust before the door
all around the ground swept clean

A ten-petaled star floating
with pastured clouds
in the moss-framed pool
plucked and placed there—
why, for what, by whom?

The black wing
that stopped her,
torn from its body,
tossed across the path,
ragged red of flesh,
white of splintered bone,
then she saw
the thick coil beyond
unblending from the dirt,
tail silent, rattles gone,
as she stared it rose up

showed the pale pleats
of its belly,
leaned and leaned
its wedged head forward,
split tongue flicking out,
bending in the air,
the slit pupils of its eyes dark
beckoning,
daring her
to step

Visions, Voices

They came to her
just before sleep or waking,
fetching the water, tending the fire
flecks, phrases of others' memories,

The patient eyes of the rabbit,
foreleg caught in the snare of split willow,

The Dauphin's secret,
he had shared only with God,
that secret Joan of Arc whispered back in his ear,
that secret now slipped into her's

The lone crow feather fallen on fresh snow
slowly covered in dusk,
a pine's lengthening shadow

The orchard prunings catching first
carrying the flame to the split rounds
the rope cramped into her wrists
her vertebrae crushed to the stake,
a tree cut too young,
first a warmth on her soles
then the seizing heat,
smoke clawing her throat,
eyes flooding over,
a salve to blur the glare, weeping,
weeping for all she would never have,
all she was leaving,
her heart searing through

The story teller's hands now still,
wings folded in her lap,
her eyes travel the circle

grip each listener
in the smoky quiet
a sigh unfurls

Those words in French,
she had sifted from the droned
hush of the waves
Nous devons tous brûler
et être né de nouveau,
"What do they mean?"
she asked the French sailor, who,
startled at her clear enunciation,
the words themselves,
puzzled a moment, said
We all must burn
and be born again

Fetching Water

She woke
from that clot of dream:
Mother walking toward the dark water,
hair loose down her back,
auburn, amber, gray,
wading in, deeper, deeper
until only her hair
fanned and floated
on the polished black

The air was hot,
her mouth was dry,
no water in the house,
she dressed and found the pail,
the handle cool across her callused palm,
the light strengthened as she walked,
bird song raining through her:
a yellow warble squeezed from brown,
a trill of garnet rising to ruby,
crow caws, star shards bursting white, white
when flint sparks steel

At the spring she dipped and filled her pail,
her dampened skirt hem,
the eddy of milky bubbles,
the fog just off the beach,
fading, clear

She lugged it down
to watch the back-lit breakers
lift to cresting curves, hold and hold, over-top,
then break,

cataracts of emerald slurred with leaf-bud green,
frothing into white cumulus, nimbus gray,
foam enswirling ankles as she turns and turns,
the pail sloshing over, in the draining wake

A psalm plumbed from deep-water blue:
Oh, rib of dust
come, be quenched
all of this is yours

Undertow

Always it seemed to call to her
and she always seeking
to cipher out its tongues

I only desired the cool wet,
my feet and ankles knew,
to surround and touch me
everywhere

That she had never learned to swim
raised no fear,
the sea so gently wooed her in

When deep as her knees
it jerked her off the sand
dragged her to the bottom
there battered on the hidden rocks
shoved to surface
she wheezed for breath
saw only miles of sea and sky

Where is the shore?
—Behind—
must turn, must turn

A surge of wave
swamped her,
seared her throat,
the current gripped her flooded skirts
and towed her out

I think, Mother will be sad
to see me home so soon

She rolled, she flailed
then fisted up
and there the shore
so close

My legs tangled,
toes so cold
nothing to grip, to pull or push,
how do sailors swim?
I am so heavy now,
Oh Lord, if you return me to your shore
I pledge to stray no more

She went under,
frenzied up,
stole back a breath,
sank again
light filtered as through a sail

I know there is no shore
I will float awhile
let the water touch me
here and here and here
then it will be done

Her forehead scraped on sand
she arched up,
raked frantically for breath,
convulsed in heaving coughs,
finally drew up her knees to rise,
scrambled from the surf
somehow stood
dripping in the prickling wind

A beach
tracks leading from the tide line
to low dunes, a wall of trees,
she stepped in them
shaking, shaking
finger tips, lips going blue

Smoke beneath the leaves
children at play
a shout

She staggered, slipped to her knees
submerged in the deepening cold
she swam
in the womb of sleep

Prodigal Daughter

Floating,
in delicious warmth
beneath a soft and amply heavy cover,
a crackling fire,
something cooking from the sea

Her eyes came open slowly
to two dark ones steady into her's
skin pressed to skin

Who is this woman
who has taken me in
who has warmed me out of Death?

The other unwrapped herself
smiled and stood
revealed her nakedness
she stretched and scratched but showed no shame
like Eve before the fall
then reached down, lifted a tunic
of soft tan skin, more supple than sail cloth,
drew it on, closed it over her breasts
then furled a skirt around her hips
bound both with a beaded belt,
turned, went into shadow

A house with a low curved roof of woven twigs
then I see no blanket covers me
instead a thick dark fur—skin of a bear!

Flung it back, leaped up
saw the peering eyes,
reddened, turned away

I hear the warning from Revelation:
Be clothed so that your nakedness
does not shame you.
I pray I may I redeem this sin

She tried to ignore her rising horror,
their gentle laughter.
The woman returned,
blouse and skirts in hand,
dry and smoky-warm,
she quickly dressed
relief when she turned,
and saw all there
were women

Food was brought
a broth of clams, baked roots,
she ate and ate,
'til her hunger sated,
strange words but easy smiles
much pointing
more laughing

It seems I know this place,
I strayed from here
and now am home again

Two men were summoned
they made signs she was to go with them
the younger one, tall and strongly built,
bare but for the flaps of skin and belt around
his hips and waist
sun-darkened,

smiled, held her eyes until she had to look away,
the one who had warmed her

placed a basket of dried fish into her hands
said some words that must be *farewell*
she curtsied an awkward thanks
so many were there
on the hard-packed ground
between the houses
all staring, staring

She went between,
the elder leading
the younger close behind her
their pace was quick
the path was wide and worn
with many others branching off
then narrowing as it entered
deep forest, the light through the leaves
such a quiet green

As we walk I wish
it was he who had warmed me
under the bearskin

Whence this wantonness?
why, how have I swallowed
its bitter water?

By turns she prayed to pass beyond temptation
then was preyed upon by thoughts of him.

After some hours the elder stopped and pointed,
they stood near the village clearing
the houses ranked up the hill
Billington, Brewster, Goodman, Carter, Brown
the goodwives at chores

I know them all
preferred chapters and verses
yet do not hold them dear
and Mother,
Mother is not there
the sun has left the hillside
I will go now
retake my place
in shadow

She turned and thanked the two
the younger one,
such a familiar stranger,
again held her eyes with his
brushed two fingers lightly down her arm
then turned

Turtle in the dust
a flower adrift among clouds
the warning wing
footprints leading home

Only Her Shoes

Only her shoes
down on the shore
stockings stuffed within
no other clothes, prints vanishing at the tide line
no body found
not the heathen basket
she had taken with her

Certainly she was dead
surely drowned this time
foolish girl, she had strayed and
now had paid

No, no one would miss her
except two widowers
an adolescent boy
who thought perhaps
in time they would...
but that
was not God's plan

Some were privately relieved
that they had found no body
no need for yet another grave
besides it was an empty husk
now only food for crabs

Oh, yes they mourned
held service even without the body
she had had her trials
whole family gone
and she barely a woman
but this was the Lord's will

a sign to them
to look within
lay bare their failings
strengthen their faith
all they could do now
was pray that her everlasting soul
be saved
and get on with the work

Before First Light

She rose in the dark
a sigh through the door
a prayer for each soul
in each house on the hill
when sure no one had awakened
only a late owl worked the clearing's edge
she followed the surf sound down

She removed her shoes
in the dry sand well above
the darker damp
stuffed her stockings into their toes
left them there
went to the water

When the first wave slapped
and flooded her calves, her knees
she leaped back
the fear roiling up again

She stood burning to run to the hill top
but held and held
steadied her heart, evened her breath
then pressed herself back into the wave swirl

She walked north
stayed only ankle deep
gripping the twine handle of the basket
its body crimped tightly by her landward arm
those few things of her mother wrapped within
enough starlight to see
the white lace of tatted foam
form and vanish, form and vanish

the tide was rising
flooding every print

Ahead she saw the owl
in steady flight toward High Cliff Point
that place she had been warned
never to go beyond

Return

Puzzling
how quickly she arrived:
around a rocky point,
a river's mouth,
but then a marsh
spread across the north
not dunes and beach,
no houses gathered there
only a long-abandoned fire pit,
weeds retaking foot-packed earth

The old nausea returned,
the futile scramble to the rail,
despair heaving up,
emptied on deserted ground,
desperately she turned
searched each compass point
for the right bearing
east across the stilled black waters of the bay
saw the pale line of North Spit
and knew
she had been drawn out beyond it
towed into open sea
then ferried farther north

The owl had hunted
over the cattails and reeds
now, circling back to her,
it veered upriver,
she followed
found a path
took it west

found another that crossed the narrowed stream
wound north along the marsh edge,
passed where young willows had been cut,
ground fog combing through their tiny stumps,
the way suddenly familiar
when she entered that quiet grove
whose canopy closed off all stars,
she stopped there, rested,
let the silence of dark trunks
seep into her
Sky graying out of black,
shuffle of wings,
a single low, croaked call
its after-tones echoing
in her throat, her lungs like
the thrum of a ship's bell through fog

She scanned the wood
a raven, perched
on a broken branch stub,
one eye intent on her,
she stood, walked near,
saw the shaggy feathers at its throat,
grasped its unblinking eye,
the heavy darkness of its beak

It croaked again,
took wing above the path,
led her on,
the way bending, forking,
north and east and north,
when sky just hinted blue
and birds began their morning psalms,

and earthy forest gave way to salty tang
and strands of fog untangled from the trees

she heard the sea
and the raven rasped
a hoarser hollowed call,
rose, was gone
beyond the luminous leaves

The path split
into many tracks,
here the rocky point,
there the forest
gaped for the river's mouth,
ahead would be the houses
but she smelled no smoke
only the acrid pinch
of long cold fires

Went warily over the low rise, saw
every house stripped of its woven mats
no roofs, no walls
only the thumb-thick bent willow frames,
each a lattice of rib bones, a turtle skeleton,
shell pried off and tossed into the weeds
they had left nothing else, except
one basket hanging from a pine bough,
bottom ripped loose, spilling even air

A jay poked around a fire pit,
flew up, charred morsel in its beak,
lit where three poles were bound,
swallowed, squalled

Dark clouds
ran against the shore
sudden lashing rain,

cold and hard with hail,
cowed her to the ground

Foolish, willful girl
not far enough, then too far
thought you had been called
believed you would enter
a garden of abundant grace
but this
this is all a godless waste
unholy wilderness
no going back,
now the only path
over the dune, across the beach,
into the ocean-sea,
a wave will slam you over,
the current drag you out,
down to the unlit deep
where eels will feast your flesh
where the shadow of shadows
will semble forth as snake
steal into you
shape from you
a second skin

Into Wilderness

She had not heard him
so quietly he came,
touched her shoulder

The squall passed
the stream of tears cut short
the sun,
even through leaves
warmed her, dried her

He took her hand
drew her up,
in his trimmed and awkward English
she came to miss and love
fingers to his heart he said,
"hear she
from yesterday,
so come,"

By the sheen of sweat
on his face and chest
his slightly speeded breath
she knew he had run all night

"I go,
she go,"
placed his fingers lightly on her sternum
"Yes?"
with his other hand he pointed to a path
that headed north and west
toward hills and hills of forest

"Yes," she said, "We shall,"

his eyes held long by hers
she pressed his hand firmly to her chest,
from deeper inland
raven croaked her call
kong kont, kong kont
they turned and followed it

Rumors

In the years after
stories welled up
of a white woman living among the Indians

Some said she was a captive, unretreived,
others said she had joined them willingly
and worse
had 'married' a heathen
this always told
for its titillating horror

No one ever
directly claimed
to having seen her
in visits to Indian camps and villages
or the praying towns

One tale surmised
the band she'd joined
had gone north, then west

Some thought it could be her
others were still certain she was dead
but they all agreed, that if true,
her soul was unredeemed
and each time a rumor flowed their way
they would pray for it again

Then the trickle stopped
and they forgot
a frayed strand of reed
in a discarded basket rotting
on the ash heap

Basketry

Over north and under east
over south and under west
repeat

A chant for the hands to follow
with reed and split willow
and thigh-rolled twine
her fingers were quick, precise
belying their fumbling start
so others now remarked with praise,
a little envy too,
how well hers were made,
called her *sister, cousin,*
even *daughter,*
when they gathered to form these
portable homes for their clothes, tools, food,
even water, if sealed with pitch,
when they had to travel fast and light

Out of the center cross
the hollow would bend up and rise
around the old stories, ravens, monsters,
the hero-giant Mauskop, Eve and Adam,
talk of husbands, of Moses in the rushes,
Noah and the flood,
how in the beginning darkness
was folded onto darkness
above the water,
how this world rides on Turtle's back,
how Judas betrayed Jesus,
how he was nailed on a cross
on a hill with two others,
like hides on trees,

and how three Marys
watched him die,
his mother Mary,
his mother's sister Mary,
and Mary Magdalene,
together they wondered, what was she to him?
then there was gossip from the east:
the threadbare peace
had torn

They packed their baskets,
walking always west
naming as they went

Old Woman Falls
the white braided cascade
vanishing into the mist above tall pines,

Valley of Many Bites
there bands and bands
of mosquitos ambushed them,
drove them into the icy river
to salve the itching,
escape the piercings

Lake Who Watched Eagles Plunge
where a circling male and female
whistled from opposite shores,
flew out over the water
rolled back and grappled talon to talon,
folded wings then dropped,
from that height
water would be like stone,

an instant before the death strike,
they loosed grip, spun apart,
opened wings and spiraled up,
whistling again from shore to shore
above the lake's bottomless eye,

Feasts of roasted venison,
weeks of boiled roots,
and there was the hill they named
Three Dead Trees
where she gentled the basket
holding her mother's things,
her still-born son
into the hollow
she had dug
in earth

In Raven's Dream

Last time fire
every tree a blur of falling flame
the seared wind that boiled the lake
Loon's scorched back
stained by drops of ash
her desperate call:
dive, dive,
Raven thought,
better to drown than burn
and dove
came through alone
every feather singed

This time flood
flying blind above the waters
now that the rains had ceased
a darkness blacker
than her feathers, her beak, her heart

One wing skimmed water
she flexed her alulae, rose,
leveled again just above tip-touch
where lift was unmatchable, effort eased
where wing stroke, heart beat
slowed, came even

She flew on and after a time
again feather tips on the trailing edge of a wing
plashed softly
was the water still rising, would it take her under?
how soon until, exhausted,
she faltered, fell?

Then above her nearly muted flight
she caught a sound
smaller than shrew speech
not Loon's lost keening
from another shore
this one drifting down
muffled by great distance
familiar yet too hushed to be kenned

She scraped out
her summoning call
kong kont, kong kont
a star pierced the roof of sky
glinted on the still face of the waters
Kong kont, kong kont
again, again she called
more stars
a tear of gray where
the sky was stitched to water
widened into white
then shred yellow
and the polished water shone

Aching wings so weary
how she yearned to land
kept on, the air as thick as water,
plash, plash
until she could only glide

Glimpsed a lump of dull water
banked
drew closer, saw
someone had swum up
from the depths

Turtle,
she remembered her from before,
her domed shell an island
a resting place, a place
to tuck her head beneath her wing
and sleep and sleep
and after sleeping
let down her egg,
warm it, turn it, wait
for the ravenous one
to chink an opening
squeeze through
demanding
to be filled

The Fire

Snow fills the low spot
between the trees
smoothes the ground

There is a stillness like sleep
a sleep without breathing, in
the smoke of the fire going out
the moistness of snow
as it touches the coals
and slips into where
the red glow is sinking

from that circle of darkness
the voice, hissing, soft, saying,
come into me
come into me
here, there is a calm,
a quiet
you have never,
you have always known
and all that
is left behind
the falling, falling
the black of charred wood,
the gray of ash

About the Author

James (Jim) Dott was born in Eugene, Oregon and grew up in Madison, Wisconsin. He is the son of a geologist and a naturalist and spent his childhood in the mountains of the west, on the southern Oregon Coast, and in the woods of Wisconsin and Michigan's Upper Peninsula. He attended the University of Wisconsin-Madison where he majored in Anthropology and Environmental Studies. After working as a U.S. Forest Service Hot Shot fire fighter, landscaper, and general laborer Jim returned to the University of Oregon to get a degree in Elementary Education. He taught in several school districts in Oregon before teaching internationally. Now retired, Jim lives with his family in Astoria, Oregon near the mouth of the Columbia River. He is the author of the poetry chapbook, *A Glossary of Memory,* an imagined memoir in twenty-six poems. His stories, essays, and poems have appeared in many print and online journals including *Blue Heron Review, Rain, Turtle Island Quarterly, Stringtown, Written River, Green Linden, Salal,* and *North Coast Squid.* You can learn more at jamesdott.com.

www.ingramcontent.com/pod-product-compliance
Lightning Source LLC
LaVergne TN
LVHW091320080426
835510LV00007B/578